ABC | ABC

delicious.

Slow

Welcome

When there's a chill in the air, only comfort food will do. *Slow* brings together 60 of our favourite cool-weather dishes – classic roasts, tender braised meats and deep, rich flavours are the order of the day.

Slow cooking doesn't have to mean spending ages in the kitchen, however. With just a little preparation and a pan popped in the oven or on the stove for a few hours, you can make something your family and friends will love.

Whether you plan to dish up chilli con carne for a crowd or slow-roasted pork belly, it's all here for you, as well as quicker midweek recipes for warming soups and hearty seafood dishes. All you need to do is fire up the stove and start creating some magic.

Happy cooking!

Valli

Contents

Soups

Vegetarian

Share Plates

Braised beef cheeks with salsa verde

750ml bottle red wine

2 tbs olive oil

2 tbs plain flour, seasoned,
    to dust

6 beef cheeks*, trimmed

2 onions, chopped

4 garlic cloves, chopped

2L (8 cups) good-quality beef
    stock

2 fresh bay leaves*

Mashed potato, to serve

Salsa verde

⅓ cup (80ml) extra virgin
    olive oil

2 cups flat-leaf parsley leaves

1 cup basil leaves

½ cup mint leaves

2 tbs Dijon mustard

2 tbs red wine vinegar

2 tbs salted capers, rinsed

2 anchovy fillets (optional)

Preheat the oven to 170°C.

Place the wine in a saucepan and simmer over medium heat for about 10 minutes or until reduced by half. Set aside.

Heat the oil in a large flameproof casserole over medium-high heat. Dust the beef cheeks in the seasoned flour. In batches, brown the beef cheeks for 2 minutes on each side until sealed, adding a little more oil if necessary. Remove and set aside.

Add the onion to the pan, reduce the heat to medium and cook, stirring, for 5 minutes or until softened. Stir in the garlic, then return the beef cheeks to the pan. Add the reduced wine, the beef stock and bay leaves. Season with salt and pepper. The meat should be completely covered with liquid, so top up with water if necessary. Cover and cook in the oven for 2½ hours or until the beef is meltingly tender.

Meanwhile, to make the salsa verde, place the ingredients in a blender and blend to form a smooth sauce. Season to taste – remember anchovies and capers are quite salty.

Remove the beef to a plate, then cover with foil to keep warm. Place the casserole over medium-high heat and simmer for 5–10 minutes until the sauce thickens. Serve the beef with the sauce, mashed potato and salsa verde. **Serves 6**

* Order beef cheeks from butchers. Fresh bay leaves are from selected greengrocers.

Braciola

2 garlic cloves

4 spring onions, chopped

¼ cup chopped flat-leaf
parsley leaves

5 slices mild salami (such as
sopressa or Hungarian
salami), roughly chopped

250g fontina* or Taleggio*
cheese, chopped

½ cup (40g) grated parmesan
cheese

½ cup (35g) fresh
breadcrumbs, toasted

⅓ cup (50g) sundried
tomatoes, drained

1.5kg piece centre-cut beef
eye fillet

⅓ cup (80ml) olive oil

350g vine-ripened cherry
tomatoes, separated into
sprigs

Place the garlic, spring onion, parsley, salami, fontina or Taleggio, parmesan, breadcrumbs and sundried tomatoes in a food processor, season with salt and pepper and pulse a few times to combine.

Cut 6 long pieces of kitchen string. Use a sharp knife to butterfly the beef fillet, slicing the fillet almost all the way through. Open the meat out like a book and pound with a rolling pin to flatten slightly. Spread the stuffing over the beef, leaving a 3cm border, then roll up from the side nearest to you. Tie with the string to secure, then enclose tightly in plastic wrap and chill for at least 1 hour, preferably overnight.

Preheat the oven to 200°C.

Heat the oil in a large frypan or flameproof roasting pan over high heat. Brown the beef on all sides, then place in the oven and roast for 25 minutes, adding the cherry tomatoes for the final 5 minutes, until the beef is medium-rare and the tomatoes have wilted slightly. Remove from the oven, cover loosely with foil and set aside to rest for 10 minutes.

Remove the string from the beef, then cut into thick slices and serve with the tomatoes. **Serves 6–8**

* Available from delis and gourmet food shops.

Steak with wild mushroom sauce

25g dried porcini
   mushrooms*
2 garlic cloves, crushed
2 tsp chopped thyme leaves
¼ cup (60ml) extra virgin
   olive oil
4 x 200g eye fillet steaks
40g unsalted butter
400g mixed mushrooms (such
   as Swiss brown and
   chestnut), sliced if large
⅓ cup (80ml) dry Marsala*
1 cup (250ml) beef
   consommé*
150g creme fraiche or light
   sour cream
2 tbs chopped flat-leaf
   parsley leaves

Garlic mash
½ cup (125ml) milk
80g unsalted butter
2 garlic cloves
1kg sebago potatoes,
   peeled, chopped

Soak the porcini in ⅓ cup (80ml) boiling water for 30 minutes to soften.

Meanwhile, combine the garlic, thyme, 2 tablespoons oil and some salt and pepper in a dish. Add the steaks, turning to coat in the mixture, then stand the steaks at room temperature to marinate while you make the mash.

For the mash, heat the milk, butter and garlic over low heat until the butter is melted, then set aside to infuse. Cook the potatoes in boiling water for 8–10 minutes until tender. Drain. Mash or pass through a ricer or mouli. Beat in the milk until smooth. Season. Keep warm.

Meanwhile, melt the butter and remaining oil in a frypan over medium-high heat. Add the mixed mushrooms and cook for 3–4 minutes until tender. Drain the porcini, reserving the soaking liquid, chop any large pieces and add to the pan of mushrooms. Cook for 1 minute, then add the Marsala and reserved liquid and cook for 3–4 minutes until reduced by half. Add the consommé and continue to cook for 6–8 minutes until the sauce is reduced by half again. Stir in the creme fraiche or sour cream, then simmer over low heat for 3–4 minutes. Season, then keep warm.

Heat a chargrill pan or barbecue on high heat. Cook the steaks for 2–3 minutes each side for medium-rare or until cooked to your liking. Rest the steaks, loosely covered, for 5 minutes. Add any resting juices and 1 tablespoon parsley to the mushroom sauce and reheat gently. Spread some garlic mash on each plate, top with the steaks and mushroom sauce, then sprinkle with the remaining parsley and serve. **Serves 4**

* Dried porcini are from gourmet food shops and greengrocers. Marsala is an Italian fortified wine available from selected bottle shops. Beef consommé is available in tetra packs from supermarkets; substitute good-quality beef stock.

Chilli for a crowd

½ cup (125ml) olive oil

1 onion, finely chopped

2 star anise

2 garlic cloves, finely
  chopped

1 small green chilli, seeds
  removed, finely chopped

1kg beef mince

2 tbs tomato paste

3 tsp ground cumin

1 tsp chilli powder

2 tsp smoked paprika
  (pimenton)

350ml red wine

1 tbs Worcestershire sauce

1½ cups (375ml) beef stock

400g can chopped tomatoes

400g can red kidney beans,
  rinsed, drained

1 long red chilli, seeds
  removed, finely shredded

Grated cheddar cheese, sour
  cream, mashed avocado
  and tortilla chips, to serve

Preheat the oven to 170°C.

Heat the oil in a large ovenproof saucepan or flameproof casserole over medium heat. Add the onion and star anise and cook, stirring, for 3–4 minutes until softened. Add the garlic and green chilli and cook, stirring, for 30 seconds or until fragrant. Add the beef and cook, breaking up any lumps with a wooden spoon, for 5–6 minutes until browned. Add the tomato paste and spices and cook, stirring, for 1–2 minutes. Pour in the wine, bring to a simmer, then cook for 4–6 minutes until reduced by half. Add the Worcestershire sauce, stock and tomatoes, then season well. Bring to the boil, then cover with a lid and transfer to the oven. Bake for 1 hour or until the chilli is reduced and thick.

Stir the beans into the chilli and top with the shredded red chilli. Serve the chilli with the cheese, sour cream, avocado and tortilla chips. **Serves 8–10**

Homestyle pies

1 tbs olive oil
1 onion, finely chopped
500g beef mince
200g mushrooms, chopped
2 tbs tomato paste
2 tbs plain flour
1 tbs Worcestershire sauce
1 cup (250ml) beef
   consommé*
2 sheets frozen shortcrust
   pastry, thawed
2 sheets frozen puff pastry,
   thawed
1 egg, beaten
Tomato sauce (ketchup),
   to serve

Mushy peas
¾ cup (185ml) chicken stock
1¼ cups (150g) frozen peas
5 mint leaves
1 tbs mascarpone or creme
   fraiche

Heat the oil in a large saucepan over medium heat. Add the onion and cook, stirring, for 3–4 minutes until soft. Add the mince and cook, stirring, for 4–5 minutes until browned. Add the mushrooms and tomato paste and cook, stirring, for a further 2–3 minutes, then stir in the flour, Worcestershire sauce and beef consommé. Bring to the boil, then reduce the heat to medium–low and simmer for 10 minutes or until the mixture has thickened. Season with sea salt and freshly ground black pepper, then allow to cool.

Preheat the oven to 200°C.

Grease 8 individual pie dishes (about 11cm long). Cut each shortcrust pastry sheet into 4 equal pieces and use to line the pie dishes. Cut each puff pastry sheet into 4 equal pieces. Fill the pies with the cooled meat mixture, then top with the puff pastry lids, pressing the edges to seal. Trim off any excess pastry, then crimp the edges with a fork or your fingers. Use the pastry trimmings to decorate the top of the pies, if desired. Brush the tops with the beaten egg, then bake for 20 minutes or until golden.

Meanwhile, make the mushy peas. Place the stock in a saucepan and bring to the boil. Add the peas and cook for 2–3 minutes until tender. Add the mint, then blend with a hand blender or use a potato masher to roughly mash. Season to taste with salt and pepper, then stir in the mascarpone or creme fraiche. Keep warm.

Serve the pies with the mushy peas and, of course, tomato sauce.

Makes 8

* Beef consommé is available in tetra packs from supermarkets. Substitute good-quality beef stock.

Chinese braised beef

2 tbs plain flour

1 tsp five-spice powder

1kg boneless beef shin*,
   cut into 5cm pieces

¼ cup (60ml) peanut or
   sunflower oil

1 onion, finely chopped

4 garlic cloves, sliced

3cm piece ginger, peeled,
   grated

½ bunch spring onions, finely
   chopped, plus extra
   shredded spring onion to
   serve

1 long red chilli, seeds
   removed, finely chopped,
   plus extra shredded
   chilli to serve

50g Chinese rock sugar*
   or brown sugar

¼ cup (60ml) Chinese rice
   wine (shaoxing)*

1 cinnamon quill

¼ cup (60ml) dark soy sauce

1L (4 cups) beef consommé

2 tbs peanut butter

2 tbs hoisin sauce

Steamed bok choy and
   steamed Chinese buns*,
   to serve

Combine the flour and five-spice powder with 1 teaspoon salt. Coat the beef in the flour mixture, shaking off and reserving any excess.

Heat 2 tablespoons oil in a flameproof casserole over medium-high heat. In batches, cook the beef, turning, for 3–4 minutes until browned all over. Remove from the pan and set aside.

Add the remaining 1 tablespoon oil to the pan and cook the onion, stirring, for 1–2 minutes until softened. Add the garlic, ginger, spring onion and chilli, then cook, stirring, for a further 1 minute. Stir in the reserved flour mixture with the sugar, rice wine, cinnamon, soy sauce, consommé, peanut butter and hoisin sauce. Return the beef to the pan, then increase the heat to medium–high and bring to the boil. Cover and transfer to the oven. Bake for 2 hours or until the beef is tender.

Top the braised beef with the shredded spring onion and chilli, then serve with the steamed bok choy and Chinese buns. **Serves 4**

* Beef shin is from butchers; substitute chuck steak. Chinese rock sugar, rice wine and buns are from Asian food shops.

Greek-style pasta bake with lamb

1 tbs olive oil

1 lamb mini roast or half leg
(about 800g)

125g sliced pancetta, cut into
strips

1 tbs chopped rosemary

150ml dry red wine

600ml tomato passata (sugo)*

600ml lamb* or chicken stock

1 tsp sugar

400g penne

280g jar marinated
artichokes, drained,
chopped

Lemon wedges, to serve

Crumbled feta, kalamata
olives and parsley, dressed
with olive oil and lemon
juice, to serve (optional)

Preheat the oven to 180°C.

Heat the oil in a large frypan over medium heat. Season the lamb all over with salt and pepper, then add to the pan and cook, turning, for 5 minutes or until browned. Remove and set aside. Add the pancetta and rosemary to the pan and cook, stirring, for 4–5 minutes until the pancetta starts to crisp. Add the wine and bring to the boil, then add the passata, stock and sugar. Season to taste, then pour the tomato mixture into a roasting pan and stir in the penne.

Set a rack over the roasting pan, then place the lamb on the rack. Bake the lamb and pasta for 40 minutes or until the lamb juices run clear when pierced with a skewer and the pasta is al dente. Set the lamb aside in a warm place to rest for 10 minutes and stir the artichoke through the pasta.

Slice the lamb and serve with the pasta and lemon to squeeze and a salad of feta, olives and parsley, if desired. **Serves 3–4**

* Passata (sieved tomatoes) is available in bottles from supermarkets. Lamb stock is available from butchers.

Oven-baked lamb curry

600g lamb fillets, cut into
  2cm cubes
2 tbs olive oil
1 onion, thinly sliced
2 tbs mild curry paste (such
  as korma)
600ml chicken or vegetable
  stock
400g can chopped tomatoes
2 cinnamon quills
2 garlic cloves, finely
  chopped
12 fresh curry leaves*
1⅓ cups (300g) medium-grain
  rice
Natural yoghurt, to serve

Preheat the oven to 180°C.

Season the lamb. Heat half the oil in a frypan over medium-high heat. Brown the lamb, in batches, for 2–3 minutes, then remove and set aside.

Return the pan to medium heat with the remaining oil. Add the onion and cook, stirring, for 5 minutes until golden. Add the curry paste and stir for a few seconds until fragrant, then transfer to a 2.5-litre (10-cup) baking dish. Add the lamb, stock, tomatoes, cinnamon, garlic and curry leaves. Season with salt and pepper, stir well to combine, then cover with foil and bake for 20 minutes.

Stir the rice into the curry, then return to the oven, uncovered, for 10 minutes or until the lamb is tender and the rice is cooked. Serve the curry topped with the yoghurt. **Serves 4**

* From selected greengrocers and Asian food shops.

Lamb and apricot tagine

2 garlic cloves, grated
½ tsp ground turmeric
1 tbs grated ginger
⅓ cup (80ml) olive oil
1kg diced lamb shoulder
20g unsalted butter
2 onions, chopped
1 cinnamon quill
1½ tbs ras el hanout*
400g can chickpeas, rinsed,
    drained
400g can chopped tomatoes
2 cups (500ml) lamb* or beef
    stock
1 tbs honey
150g dried apricots
2 tbs sesame seeds, toasted

Couscous
¼ cup (60ml) olive oil
1 onion, finely chopped
Grated zest of 1½ oranges
½ cup currants
2 tsp smoked paprika
    (pimenton)
2 tsp ground cumin
1 cup (250ml) orange juice
50g unsalted butter
2 cups (400g) couscous
2 tbs chopped coriander
    (optional)

Combine the garlic, turmeric, ginger and 2 tablespoons oil in a bowl. Add the lamb, turning to coat in the mixture. Cover and place in the fridge to marinate for 1 hour.

Heat the remaining 2 tablespoons oil in a flameproof casserole over medium-high heat. In batches, seal the lamb for 2–3 minutes, turning until browned on all sides. Set aside.

Melt the butter in the same pan over medium–low heat. Add the onion and cook, stirring occasionally, for 5 minutes or until softened. Add the cinnamon and ras el hanout, then return the lamb to the pan and gently toss to coat in the spices. Add the chickpeas, tomatoes, stock and honey – you should have just enough liquid to cover the lamb. Increase the heat to medium–high, bring to a simmer, then reduce the heat to low and simmer, partially covered, for 45 minutes. Uncover and simmer for 30 minutes, stirring occasionally, then add the apricots and simmer for a further 10–15 minutes until the lamb is tender and the sauce is rich.

For the couscous, heat the oil in a saucepan over low heat. Add the onion, zest, currants and spices. Cook, stirring occasionally, for 10 minutes or until the onion is soft. In a separate pan, bring the juice, butter and 1 cup (250ml) water to the boil, then slowly add the couscous. Remove from the heat and stand, covered, for 5 minutes. Fluff with a fork, then stir in the onion mixture and coriander, if desired. Serve the tagine, scattered with the sesame seeds, with the couscous. **Serves 4**

* Ras el hanout (a Moroccan spice blend) is from Middle Eastern and gourmet shops. Lamb stock is available from butchers.

Massaman curry lamb shanks

2 tbs sunflower oil

6 French-trimmed lamb
  shanks

1 onion, finely chopped

⅓ cup (100g) massaman curry
  paste

1 tbs grated palm sugar* or
  brown sugar

3 kaffir lime leaves*

400ml coconut cream

2 cups (500ml) beef stock

500g baby chat potatoes,
  peeled, halved if large

1 cup (120g) frozen peas

2 tbs lime juice

2 tbs fish sauce

Coriander leaves and
  steamed jasmine rice,
  to serve

Preheat the oven to 180°C.

Heat 1 tablespoon oil in a large flameproof casserole over medium-high heat. Season the lamb shanks, then, in batches, cook the lamb, turning, for 3–4 minutes until browned all over. Set the shanks aside.

Reduce the heat to medium, then add the remaining 1 tablespoon oil to the pan. Cook the onion, stirring, for 2–3 minutes until softened. Add the curry paste and cook, stirring, for 1–2 minutes until fragrant. Stir in the sugar, lime leaves, coconut cream and stock, then return the lamb to the pan. Increase the heat to high and bring to the boil. Cover, then transfer to the oven. Bake for 1 hour.

Add the potato to the pan and cook for a further 30 minutes or until the lamb and potatoes are tender. Add the peas and bake for a further 10 minutes or until the peas are tender.

Stir through the lime juice and fish sauce and season to taste. Serve the lamb shanks with the coriander and steamed rice.
Serves 6

* Palm sugar and kaffir lime leaves are from Asian food shops.

Bobotie

¼ cup (40g) sultanas

¼ cup (60ml) brandy

2 tbs olive oil

2 onions, chopped

2 garlic cloves, finely chopped

1kg lamb mince

2 tbs mild curry powder

½ cup (125ml) tomato puree or passata (sugo)

3 tbs apricot jam

4 eggs, plus 2 egg yolks

600ml thickened cream

½ tsp caster sugar

Green salad, to serve

Soak the sultanas in 2 tablespoons brandy for 2 hours.

Preheat the oven to 180°C.

Heat the oil in a saucepan over medium heat. Add the onion and cook, stirring, for 2–3 minutes until starting to soften. Add the garlic and cook for a further 1 minute until softened, then add the lamb and cook, stirring, for 6–8 minutes until browned. Add the curry powder, tomato puree or passata and jam, then continue to cook over low heat for 3–4 minutes until the lamb is cooked through. Stir in the sultanas and soaking liquid, then spread into a 20cm x 30cm baking dish.

Beat the eggs, egg yolks and cream with some salt and pepper, then whisk in the sugar and the remaining 1 tablespoon brandy until combined. Strain through a sieve over the lamb. Place the baking dish in a roasting pan, then pour enough boiling water into the pan to come halfway up the sides of the baking dish. Bake in the oven for 40 minutes or until the topping is set and golden. Serve with a green salad. **Serves 6–8**

Lamb en croute

30g unsalted butter

150g Swiss brown
  mushrooms, chopped

3 chicken livers, trimmed,
  finely chopped

4 eschalots, finely chopped

2 garlic cloves, finely
  chopped

1½ bunches English spinach,
  chopped

2 tbs toasted pine nuts,
  chopped

2 tbs olive oil

2 x 200g lamb backstraps,
  trimmed

1 cup (250ml) red wine

1 cup (250ml) beef
  or veal stock*

¼ cup (80g) redcurrant jelly

2 sheets frozen puff pastry,
  thawed

1 egg, lightly beaten

Steamed green beans,
  to serve

Preheat the oven to 200°C.

Melt the butter in a frypan over medium-high heat. Add the mushrooms, chicken liver, eschalot and garlic to the pan, and cook for 2–3 minutes until the mushrooms are softened and the liver is sealed. Add the spinach and cook, stirring, for 1 minute or until wilted. Season and cool slightly. Transfer to a food processor, pulse a few times to form a coarse paste, then stir through the pine nuts. Transfer to a bowl, cover and refrigerate until cold.

Heat the oil in a frypan over high heat. Season the lamb, then add to the pan and cook, turning once, for 2–3 minutes or until brown all over. Remove from the pan and set aside to cool.

Add the red wine to the pan and simmer for 2–3 minutes until slightly reduced. Add the stock and redcurrant jelly and cook, stirring, for 5–6 minutes or until reduced and thick. Keep warm.

Spread one-quarter of the spinach mixture over two-thirds of 1 puff pastry sheet, leaving a 3cm border. Place 1 lamb backstrap on the spinach mixture, then cover the lamb with another quarter of the spinach mixture. Tuck in the sides of the pastry, then fold over the pastry to enclose the filling. Trim the pastry, then press down to seal the edges. Repeat with the remaining pastry, spinach mixture and lamb.

Cut any excess pastry into leaf shapes, if desired, and place on top of the lamb parcels. Brush the pastry with the egg. Place on a baking tray and bake for 12–15 minutes until golden. Remove from the oven and set aside to rest for 5 minutes.

Slice the lamb en croute and serve with the redcurrant sauce and steamed green beans. **Serves 4**

* Veal stock is from selected delis and butchers.

Radicchio and gorgonzola risotto

1L (4 cups) chicken or
vegetable stock
2 cups (500ml) dry white wine
60g unsalted butter
⅓ cup (80ml) olive oil
1 onion, finely chopped
2 garlic cloves, thinly sliced
400g arborio rice
2 fresh bay leaves*
1 radicchio, outer leaves
discarded, inner leaves
roughly torn
1¾ cups (140g) finely grated
parmesan cheese, plus
extra to serve
2 tbs chopped flat-leaf
parsley leaves
150g gorgonzola dolce or
other mild creamy blue
cheese, crumbled

Place the stock and wine in a saucepan and bring to the boil, then keep warm over low heat.

Place the butter and oil in a deep frypan over medium–low heat. Add the onion and garlic and cook, stirring, for 2–3 minutes until softened. Add the rice and bay leaves and cook, stirring, for 2 minutes to coat the grains.

Stir in the stock mixture, a ladleful at a time, allowing each to be absorbed before adding the next. Continue to cook, stirring frequently, until all the stock has been absorbed and the rice is al dente – this should take about 20 minutes.

Fold through the radicchio, parmesan, parsley and half the gorgonzola, then stand for 2 minutes or until the cheese has melted and the radicchio has wilted slightly.

Divide the risotto among serving plates, then serve scattered with the remaining gorgonzola and extra parmesan. **Serves 6**

* Fresh bay leaves are from selected greengrocers.

Deconstructed lasagne

2 tbs olive oil

2 onions, chopped

2 garlic cloves, chopped

1 tbs chopped rosemary

½ tsp dried chilli flakes

Grated zest of 1 lemon

¼ cup salted capers, rinsed,
   chopped

4 tbs (⅓ cup) tomato paste

600g beef mince

2 tbs balsamic vinegar

½ cup pitted kalamata olives,
   chopped

½ cup flat-leaf parsley leaves,
   chopped, plus 2 tbs extra
   for the ricotta

2 x 400g cans chopped
   tomatoes

500g lasagnette pasta*

1 cup (240g) fresh ricotta

½ cup (40g) grated parmesan
   cheese, plus extra to serve

Heat the oil in a saucepan over medium–low heat. Add the onion, garlic and rosemary and cook, stirring occasionally, for 2–3 minutes until softened. Add the chilli flakes, lemon zest and capers and cook for a further minute, then add the tomato paste and cook, stirring, for 30 seconds. Add the beef and cook, breaking up with a wooden spoon, for 3–4 minutes until browned. Add the balsamic, olives, parsley and tomatoes. Season with salt and pepper, bring to a simmer, then reduce the heat to low and cook, stirring occasionally, for 30–40 minutes until thick and rich.

When the sauce is almost ready, cook the pasta in a large saucepan of boiling, salted water according to the packet instructions. Drain, then toss with the sauce.

Stir the extra parsley through the ricotta. Season, then place a dollop of ricotta in the base of 4–6 bowls. Top with the pasta, sprinkle with the parmesan, then add another dollop of ricotta and serve. **Serves 4–6**

* Lasagnette is a long, wide, curly-edged pasta, from gourmet shops and delis. Substitute another long, wide pasta, such as pappardelle.

Taleggio, pea and pancetta pasta bake

400g large pasta shells
(conchiglioni)*
2 tbs olive oil, plus extra to
toss
1¾ cups (210g) peas
2 large zucchini
100g pancetta or bacon,
finely chopped
1 garlic clove, grated
Grated zest of 1 lemon
500g Taleggio cheese*,
chopped
300ml thickened cream
Pinch of grated nutmeg
¼ cup (20g) grated parmesan

Preheat the oven to 180°C and grease a large baking dish.

Cook the pasta shells in boiling, salted water according to the packet instructions until just tender. Drain, then refresh and toss in a little olive oil.

Meanwhile, cook the peas in boiling water for 2–3 minutes until tender. Drain and refresh. Coarsely grate the zucchini. Place the zucchini in a colander, sprinkle with salt, then set aside for 10 minutes. Rinse and pat dry.

Heat the oil in a frypan over medium heat. Add the pancetta or bacon and cook, stirring, for 2–3 minutes until starting to crisp. Add the garlic, zucchini and lemon zest, then cook for a further 2 minutes. Season. Cool slightly, then place in a food processor with the peas and pulse to a coarse paste. Alternatively, roughly mash with a fork. Fill the pasta shells with the pea mixture, then arrange in the baking dish.

Place the Taleggio and cream in a heatproof bowl set over a pan of simmering water, stirring occasionally, until the cheese has melted and the sauce is smooth. Season with the nutmeg, salt and pepper. Pour the sauce over the pasta shells and sprinkle with the parmesan. Bake in the oven for 20 minutes until golden and bubbling. **Serves 6–8**

* Taleggio is an Italian washed-rind cheese from delis and gourmet food shops.

Macaroni cheese with truffle oil

400g macaroni

2–3 tbs truffle oil* (to taste),
plus extra to serve

1 tbs olive oil

2 eschalots, finely chopped

4 bacon rashers, finely
chopped

2 garlic cloves, finely
chopped

1 tsp fresh thyme leaves

1½ cups (375ml) thickened
cream

3 cups (360g) grated
good-quality cheddar
cheese

⅓ cup (25g) grated parmesan
cheese

Grilled bread and chopped
flat-leaf parsley leaves, to
serve

Preheat the oven to 180°C and grease a 1-litre (4-cup) baking dish.

Cook the pasta in a large pan of boiling, salted water according to the packet instructions. Drain, then return to the pan, toss with the truffle oil to taste and season.

Meanwhile, heat the olive oil in a large, deep frypan over medium heat. Add the eschalot, bacon and garlic and cook, stirring, for 2–3 minutes until the eschalot softens. Add the thyme leaves and cream, then simmer for 3 minutes until thickened slightly. Add the pasta and three-quarters of the cheddar to the sauce, stirring to coat.

Pile the mixture into the prepared baking dish, then scatter with the parmesan and remaining cheddar. Bake for 30 minutes or until bubbling and golden. Sprinkle with the parsley, drizzle with a little extra truffle oil if desired, then serve with the grilled bread.

Serves 4

* Truffle oil is from gourmet food shops and delis.

Make-ahead lasagne

1 tbs olive oil

500g beef mince

500g fresh ricotta

2 eggs, lightly beaten

1 cup basil leaves, chopped

1½ cups (120g) finely grated
   parmesan cheese

375g fresh lasagne sheets

600ml good-quality tomato
   pasta sauce

250g grated mozzarella
   cheese

250g bocconcini, thinly sliced

Preheat the oven to 180°C. Grease a 22cm x 33cm baking dish.

Place the oil in a non-stick frypan over medium heat. Add the beef and cook, breaking up any lumps with a wooden spoon, for 6–8 minutes until browned. Set aside.

Combine the ricotta, eggs, basil and half the parmesan in a bowl and season. Set aside.

Line the prepared baking dish with one-third of the lasagne sheets. Spread with one-third of the pasta sauce, then top with half the ricotta mixture and half the meat. Sprinkle with half the grated mozzarella. Repeat the layers, then top with the remaining pasta sheets and spread with the remaining pasta sauce. Arrange the sliced bocconcini on top, then sprinkle with the remaining parmesan. Cover with a layer of baking paper and a layer of foil. (If you like, you can pop the lasagne in the fridge at this stage and keep for up to 1 day.)

Bake the lasagne for 30 minutes, then remove the foil and baking paper and bake for a further 20 minutes or until the lasagne is bubbling and golden. Stand for 15 minutes, then cut into slices and serve. **Serves 6–8**

Beetroot risotto with melting brie

350g beetroot, peeled,
cut into 1cm cubes

1L (4 cups) chicken or
vegetable stock

1 tbs olive oil

1 onion, finely chopped

3 garlic cloves, chopped

250g arborio rice

100ml white wine

50g unsalted butter

A few thyme sprigs, leaves
picked

1¼ cups (100g) finely grated
parmesan cheese, plus
extra to serve

120g buche d'Affinois or
other ripe double-cream
brie, thickly sliced

Mixed micro herbs* or extra
thyme leaves, to serve

Place the beetroot and stock in a saucepan, bring to a simmer over medium heat and cook for 10–15 minutes until the beetroot is tender. Drain the beetroot, reserving the stock. Set the beetroot aside. Return the stock to the pan and place over low heat.

Meanwhile, heat the oil in a separate saucepan over medium–low heat. Add the onion and cook, stirring, for 1–2 minutes until softened. Add the garlic and rice, stirring for 1–2 minutes to coat the grains, then add the wine and allow to bubble until almost evaporated.

Stir in the stock, a ladleful at a time, allowing each to be absorbed before adding the next. Continue to cook, stirring constantly, until all the stock has been absorbed and the rice is al dente – this should take about 20 minutes. Stir in the reserved beetroot.

Remove the pan from the heat. Stir in the butter, thyme leaves and parmesan, then season. Stand for 2 minutes, then divide the risotto among shallow bowls. Sprinkle with the extra parmesan and top with a slice of brie, allowing it to melt slightly. Sprinkle with the herbs and serve. **Serves 4–6**

* Micro herbs are from farmers' markets and selected greengrocers.

Roast pork with Marsala and fig sauce

1.5kg rack of pork
100ml olive oil, plus extra
   to fry
1 large red onion, cut into
   wedges
6–8 fresh figs, base scored
20 sage leaves
1 tbs plain flour
2 tsp Dijon mustard
⅓ cup (80ml) dry Marsala*
1½ cups (375ml) chicken
   stock
½ cup fig jam*, plus extra
   to serve

Preheat the oven to 240°C.

Score the pork rind at 2cm intervals, then rub with 2 tablespoons oil and sprinkle with sea salt. Place on a rack in a large roasting pan and roast for 15 minutes. Reduce the heat to 200°C, add the onion and cook for a further 1 hour or until the skin is crisp and the pork is cooked through, adding the figs for the final 5 minutes.

Meanwhile, heat the remaining 3 tablespoons oil in a small frypan over high heat. Add the sage leaves and fry for 1 minute until crisp, then remove with a slotted spoon and drain on paper towel.

Remove the pork, figs and onion from the roasting pan and place on a platter to rest, covered, while you make the sauce. Drain all but 1 tablespoon of fat from the roasting pan, then place the pan over medium heat. Add the flour and stir until combined. Whisk in the mustard, then the Marsala and stock. Bring to a simmer over medium heat, then add the jam and stir until combined. Cook, stirring occasionally, for 5–6 minutes until thickened. (You can strain the sauce at this stage, but I like to leave it a little chunky.)

Carve the pork and serve with the onion, figs, fried sage leaves, fig sauce and extra fig jam. **Serves 6**

* Marsala is an Italian fortified wine available from selected bottle shops. Fig jam is available from gourmet food shops.

Meatballs with heavenly mash

250g pork mince

250g veal mince

250g lamb mince

4 garlic cloves, finely
  chopped

2 tbs fresh breadcrumbs

1 egg, lightly beaten

½ cup (120g) fresh ricotta

¼ cup (20g) grated parmesan
  cheese

¼ cup chopped flat-leaf
  parsley leaves, plus extra
  to serve

¼ cup finely chopped basil

¼ cup (60ml) olive oil

1 onion, finely chopped

1 anchovy fillet in oil, drained

750ml bottle tomato passata
  (sugo)

400g can chopped tomatoes

2 tsp caster sugar

Heavenly mash

1kg potatoes, peeled,
  chopped

½ cup (125ml) milk

½ cup (125ml) pure (thin)
  cream

1 cup (100g) grated fontina
  or other melting cheese

Unsalted butter, to serve

Place the mince, garlic, breadcrumbs, egg, ricotta, parmesan, parsley and basil in a bowl. Season well and use your hands to bring the mixture together. Shape into walnut-sized balls and chill for 30 minutes.

Heat 1 tablespoon olive oil in a large, deep frypan over medium-high heat. In batches, cook the meatballs, turning, for 3–4 minutes until browned. Set aside.

Heat the remaining 2 tablespoons oil in the same pan over medium heat. Cook the onion, stirring, for 2–3 minutes until softened. Add the anchovy, passata, chopped tomatoes and sugar, bring to a simmer, then reduce the heat to low and cook for 5–6 minutes until slightly reduced. Add the meatballs and simmer for a further 5–6 minutes until the sauce is thick and the meatballs are cooked through.

Meanwhile, for the mash, cook the potatoes in boiling, salted water for 10–12 minutes until tender. Drain, then mash until smooth. Place the milk and cream in a small saucepan over medium-high heat and bring to just below boiling point. Beat the milk mixture into the potatoes with a wooden spoon until smooth. Stir through the fontina, season, then top with a knob of butter.

Sprinkle the meatballs with the extra parsley and serve with the heavenly mash. **Serves 4–6**

Sticky pork ribs

1 tbs grated ginger

2 garlic cloves, grated

2 tbs plum sauce*

1 tbs tomato sauce (ketchup)

1 tsp dried chilli flakes

1 tbs maple syrup

1 tbs treacle

2 tbs olive oil

1.5kg pork spare ribs
  (2 racks)

Lemon wedges, to serve

Coriander leaves, to garnish

Combine the ginger, garlic, plum sauce, tomato sauce, chilli flakes, maple syrup, treacle and olive oil in a large, deep-sided tray or dish. Add the pork ribs and baste thoroughly in the marinade. Cover with plastic wrap, then marinate in the fridge for 1 hour.

Preheat the oven to 190°C and line a large baking tray with baking paper.

Place the ribs on the baking tray, reserving any of the marinade. Bake in the oven for 30 minutes, then remove from the oven and baste with the reserved marinade. Return to the oven for a further 40 minutes or until the meat is tender and the marinade is sticky and caramelised. Serve with the lemon wedges, garnished with the coriander. **Serves 4**

* Plum sauce is from Asian food shops and selected supermarkets.

Sausages with home-style baked beans

1 cup (250ml) dry white wine

2 cups (500ml) tomato puree

1 cup (250ml) good-quality
   barbecue sauce*

2 tbs brown sugar

1 tbs molasses

1 tbs Dijon mustard

2 x 400g cans cannellini
   beans, rinsed, drained

1 Toulouse sausage* or
   12 thin pork sausages

Rocket leaves, to serve

Combine the wine, tomato puree, barbecue sauce, sugar, molasses and mustard in a saucepan over medium–low heat and simmer, stirring occasionally, for 6–8 minutes until reduced by half. Add the beans to the sauce and cook for a further 10 minutes until the mixture thickens.

Meanwhile, heat a lightly oiled chargrill pan, frypan or barbecue on medium heat and cook the Toulouse sausage for 5–6 minutes each side until cooked through. (Or cook the thin pork sausages, in batches, for 8–10 minutes until browned and cooked through.)

Cut the Toulouse sausage into 4 pieces, then serve with the baked beans and rocket leaves. **Serves 4**

* Good-quality barbecue sauce is from gourmet food shops and delis. Toulouse sausage is a long, coiled French pork sausage, available from selected butchers.

Ham-hock terrine with fresh piccalilli

4 ham hocks*
1 onion, finely chopped
1 carrot, finely chopped
1 cup (250ml) dry white wine
4 thyme sprigs
6 black peppercorns
1 cup flat-leaf parsley leaves,
    finely chopped, plus extra
    sprigs, to serve
4 gold-strength gelatine
    leaves*
Baguette, cornichons and
    butter, to serve

Piccalilli
¼ cup (55g) caster sugar
½ tsp ground turmeric
¼ cup (60ml) white wine
    vinegar
300g small cauliflower florets
150g small green beans
1 red capsicum, thinly sliced
1 yellow capsicum, thinly
    sliced
1 onion, thinly sliced
1 tbs English mustard powder
1 long red chilli, seeds
    removed, sliced

Line a 1-litre (4-cup) terrine with plastic wrap, leaving plenty overhanging the sides.

Place the ham hocks, onion, carrot, wine, thyme and peppercorns in a large pan. Cover with cold water and bring to the boil. Reduce the heat to low and simmer for 3 hours, skimming occasionally, then remove from the heat and leave to cool. Once cool, remove the ham hocks and reserve 1 cup (250ml) cooking stock. Flake the meat from the hocks, discarding the skin and bones, then mix the meat with the parsley. Reheat the reserved cooking stock over low heat.

Meanwhile, soak the gelatine leaves in cold water for 5 minutes to soften. Squeeze to remove excess liquid, then add the leaves to the warmed stock and stir to dissolve.

Pack the meat into the terrine and cover with the liquid. Cover with the overhanging plastic, then chill for 2 hours to set slightly. Top with a piece of cardboard cut to fit the top of the terrine, and weigh down with unopened cans. Chill for at least 8 hours, preferably overnight, until set.

For the piccalilli, place the sugar, turmeric and vinegar in a saucepan over low heat, stirring to dissolve the sugar. Set aside. Blanch the cauliflower in boiling, salted water for 2 minutes, then add the beans and cook for a further minute. Drain, then refresh in cold water. Once cool, toss in a bowl with the vinegar mixture and remaining ingredients. Chill for 2–3 hours or until ready to serve.

Remove the terrine from the mould, garnish with the parsley sprigs, then slice and serve with the baguette, cornichons, butter and piccalilli. **Serves 4–6**

* Ham hocks are from delis and butchers. Gelatine leaves are from gourmet shops and delis.

Pork and fennel tray bake with Moroccan spice

2 x 400g pork fillets,
   trimmed, cut into thirds
3 large potatoes, cut into
   wedges
3 small fennel bulbs,
   trimmed, cut into quarters
3 red onions, cut into
   quarters
1 tbs olive oil
Thick Greek-style yoghurt,
   seasoned with salt and
   pepper, to serve

Marinade

2 preserved lemon quarters*,
   flesh and white pith
   removed, rind thinly sliced
1 garlic clove, chopped
1 small red chilli, seeds
   removed, chopped
1 tsp smoked paprika
   (pimenton)
1 tsp ground cumin
1 tbs honey
1 cup coriander leaves, plus
   extra to serve
¼ cup (60ml) olive oil

Preheat the oven to 190°C and grease a large roasting pan.

For the marinade, place all the ingredients in a small food processor, season, then whiz into a paste.

Coat the pork in the paste, then set aside to marinate while you prepare the vegetables.

Place the potato and fennel in a saucepan of cold, salted water. Bring to the boil over medium heat, then cook for 5 minutes to par-boil. Drain, then place in the roasting pan with the onion. Drizzle with oil, season, then roast for 20 minutes or until just tender.

Add the pork to the roasting pan and toss well with the vegetables. Roast for 20–25 minutes until the pork is cooked. Transfer the pork to a plate and rest, loosely covered with foil, for 10 minutes.

Increase the oven to 220°C.

Return the vegetables to the oven for a further 10 minutes or until caramelised and crisp.

Serve the vegetables with the pork, seasoned yoghurt and extra coriander leaves. **Serves 4–6**

* Available from delis and gourmet food shops.

Eight-hour pork belly with caramelised peanut and chilli relish

1.5kg boneless pork belly
 (skin on)
Sunflower oil, to rub
1 tbs sea salt
Steamed bok choy, to serve

Caramelised peanut
and chilli relish
¼ cup (60ml) peanut oil
2 garlic cloves, chopped
1 long red chilli, seeds
 removed, chopped
4 Asian (red) eschalots*,
 chopped
2 tsp caster sugar
2 tbs unsalted peanuts
½ tsp ground coriander
1 tbs sesame oil
1 tbs soy sauce
Juice of 1 lime
2 tbs finely chopped
 coriander, plus extra
 to serve

Preheat the oven to 100°C or its lowest temperature.

Score the pork skin and fat in a criss-cross pattern, without cutting into the meat. Place the pork on a rack in the sink and pour over a kettle of boiling water (this will result in crisp crackling). Dry well with paper towel, then rub the pork skin with the sunflower oil and salt.

Place the pork, skin-side up, on a rack set in a roasting pan and pour in 200ml water. Roast for 8 hours or until very tender.

Increase the oven to 220°C. Roast the pork for a further 20 minutes or until the crackling is crisp.

Meanwhile, for the relish, heat 1 tablespoon peanut oil in a small frypan over medium-high heat. Cook the garlic and chilli, stirring, for 1–2 minutes until fragrant. Stir in the eschalot and sugar, then cook for 3–4 minutes until the sugar starts to caramelise. Add the peanuts and ground coriander, then cook, stirring, for 1–2 minutes to coat the peanuts. Transfer the mixture to a mortar and pestle and pound into a coarse paste. Stir in the remaining ingredients and 2–3 tablespoons water. Transfer to a serving bowl.

Slice the pork belly, garnish with the coriander leaves and serve with the bok choy and relish. **Serves 4–6**

* From Asian food shops and selected greengrocers.

Frankfurts with stir-fried red cabbage

8 good-quality Continental
  frankfurts
1 tbs sunflower oil
30g unsalted butter
1 red onion, thinly sliced
1 green apple, peeled, sliced
1 garlic clove, chopped
400g red cabbage, thinly
  sliced
2 tbs red wine vinegar
2 tbs apple and sage jelly*
  or redcurrant jelly
1 tbs chopped flat-leaf
  parsley leaves
Rye bread (optional), to serve

Heat a chargrill pan or frypan over medium heat and cook frankfurts for 2–3 minutes, turning, until heated through. (Or simmer in a saucepan of boiling water for 3–4 minutes.)

Heat the oil and butter in a wok or deep frypan over medium heat. Add the onion, apple and garlic and stir-fry for 2–3 minutes until the onion just softens. Add the cabbage and stir-fry for 2–3 minutes until wilted. Stir in the vinegar, jelly and parsley, then season and heat through. Transfer to a platter or large serving dish and toss with the frankfurts. Serve with the rye bread, if desired.

Serves 4

* Apple and sage jelly is from gourmet food shops.

Pork chops with wild mushroom sauce and balsamic potatoes

⅓ cup (80ml) olive oil

1kg chat potatoes, halved

4 small red onions, halved or quartered

1 garlic bulb, halved horizontally

⅔ cup (160ml) balsamic vinegar

½ cup sage leaves, roughly chopped

125g unsalted butter

10g dried porcini mushrooms*

4 x 200g pork cutlets

150g mixed wild mushrooms (such as chestnuts, morels and chanterelles), halved or sliced if large

¾ cup (185ml) dry Marsala*

½ cup (125ml) beef consommé

2 tbs chopped flat-leaf parsley leaves, plus extra sprigs to serve

Preheat the oven to 180°C.

Heat 2 tablespoons olive oil in a large ovenproof frypan over medium heat. Season the potatoes and cook, cut-side down, for 10 minutes until golden and crispy. Add the onion, garlic, balsamic vinegar, sage and half the butter. Season, then transfer to the oven to cook, turning once, for 25 minutes or until the vegetables are tender and caramelised.

Meanwhile, soak the porcini in ½ cup (125ml) boiling water for 10 minutes. Drain, reserving the soaking liquid, then roughly chop the porcini and set aside.

Place 1 tablespoon olive oil in a clean frypan over medium heat. Season the pork and cook for 5–6 minutes each side until golden and cooked through. Transfer to a plate and rest, loosely covered with foil, while you make the sauce.

Return the frypan to medium–high heat and add the remaining 1 tablespoon oil. Add the wild mushrooms and chopped porcini to the pan, season and cook, stirring, for 3–4 minutes until softened. Remove the mushrooms from the pan and set aside. Add the Marsala, consommé and reserved soaking liquid to the pan. Bring to a simmer and cook for 5–6 minutes until reduced. Return the mushrooms to the pan. Chop the remaining butter into small pieces, then gradually whisk the butter into the sauce until it is thick and glossy.

Divide the pork among serving plates, drizzle with the sauce and scatter with the chopped parsley. Garnish the balsamic roasted potatoes with the parsley sprigs, then serve with the pork. **Serves 4**

* Dried porcini are from gourmet food shops and delis. Marsala is an Italian fortified wine from bottle shops.

Roast chicken with pan-roasted romesco

⅓ cup (80ml) olive oil

1 tbs smoked paprika (pimenton)

1 tbs chopped rosemary leaves

8 garlic cloves

1.8kg free-range chicken

1 red capsicum, cut into chunks

1 tomato, cut into chunks

½ cup (80g) blanched almonds, toasted

¼ cup (15g) fresh breadcrumbs, lightly oven-toasted

¼ cup chopped flat-leaf parsley leaves

1 cup (250ml) dry sherry

Combine 2 tablespoons oil with the paprika, rosemary and 2 crushed garlic cloves in a bowl. Season, then rub the mixture over the chicken. Cover and marinate in the fridge for 30 minutes.

Preheat the oven to 180°C.

Place the chicken in a roasting pan and roast for 1 hour. Scatter the capsicum, tomato and remaining garlic cloves around the chicken and drizzle with the remaining oil. Roast for a further 20 minutes or until the chicken is golden and cooked (the juices run clear when the thigh is pierced) and the vegetables have softened.

Meanwhile, place the almonds, breadcrumbs and parsley in a food processor. Season and process until combined. Set aside.

Remove the chicken to a plate, cover loosely with foil and leave to rest while you finish the sauce. Place the roasting pan with the vegetables over medium heat, add the sherry and cook, stirring, for 5 minutes until slightly reduced. Cool slightly, then place in a food processor with half the crumb mixture and process until smooth. Season with salt and pepper.

Serve the roast chicken on a platter or board sprinkled with the remaining crumb mixture, with the romesco sauce on the side.

Serves 4

Roast quail with split pea dhal

2 tbs sunflower oil

1 tsp ground cardamom

1 tsp ground cumin

Pinch of cayenne pepper

6 quails*, butterflied (ask
your butcher to do this)

150g green beans, blanched

Curry butter and coriander
sprigs, to serve

Curry butter

2 tsp olive oil

6 eschalots, finely chopped

2 tsp curry powder

1 tbs white wine vinegar

1 tbs tomato kasundi*
(optional)

2 tbs chopped coriander
leaves

200g unsalted butter,
softened

Split pea dhal

300g dried yellow split peas

2 tbs sunflower oil

1 onion, finely chopped

1 tbs panch phora*

For the curry butter, place the oil in a frypan over low heat. Cook the eschalot, stirring, for 1–2 minutes until soft. Add curry powder and cook, stirring, for 30 seconds or until fragrant. Stir in the vinegar and kasundi and cook for 1 minute or until the liquid has evaporated. Cool, then mix well with the coriander and butter.

Spoon onto plastic wrap, then shape into a log and enclose. Freeze until firm.

For the dhal, soak the split peas in cold water for 2 hours, then drain. Place the oil in a saucepan over low heat. Cook the onion, stirring, for 2–3 minutes until softened. Stir in the panch phora, then add the split peas and 3 cups (750ml) water. Bring to a simmer, then reduce the heat to low and cook, stirring occasionally, for 1–1¼ hours until the split peas are soft, topping up with more water if the mixture becomes too dry. Beat with a wooden spoon, then season and keep warm.

Meanwhile, preheat the oven to 190°C.

Rub the oil and spices over the quails, then season. In batches, cook the quails, skin-side down, in a frypan over medium-high heat for 2–3 minutes until starting to brown. Transfer the quails to a baking tray, skin-side up, and roast for 8 minutes or until just cooked. Rest, loosely covered with foil, for 5 minutes.

Pile the dhal onto plates and top with the beans and a quail. Top each quail with a slice of curry butter and serve garnished with the coriander. **Serves 6**

* Quail is from selected butchers and poultry shops. Tomato kasundi is from gourmet food shops. Panch phora (a mixture of fennel, cumin, nigella seeds, fenugreek and mustard seeds) is available from Indian gourmet food shops.

Oven-baked Thai chicken curry

1 tbs sunflower oil

1 onion, finely chopped

2 large (180–200g) free-range
chicken breast fillets, cut
into 2cm pieces

4 tbs Thai green curry paste
(or to taste)

1¼ cups (250g) jasmine rice

Zest and juice of 1 lime

400ml coconut milk

1 lemongrass stem, bruised

3 kaffir lime leaves*, finely
shredded

250g cherry tomatoes, halved
if large

1 long red chilli, seeds
removed, sliced

Coriander sprigs, Thai basil
leaves*, fried Asian
shallots* and creme fraiche
or sour cream, to serve

Preheat the oven to 200°C.

Heat the oil in a wide flameproof casserole over medium heat.
Add the onion and cook for 1–2 minutes until slightly softened. Add
the chicken and curry paste, then cook, stirring, for 3–5 minutes
until the chicken is just starting to brown and the paste is fragrant.

Add the rice, lime zest and juice, coconut milk, lemongrass, kaffir
lime leaves (reserving a little to garnish) and 1 cup (250ml) water.
Bring to the boil, then cover and bake in the oven for 15 minutes or
until the chicken is cooked and the rice is tender, adding the
tomatoes for the final 5 minutes of cooking time.

Stand, covered, for 5 minutes, then stir well and serve in bowls
topped with the sliced chilli, herbs, fried shallots and a dollop of
creme fraiche or sour cream. **Serves 4–6**

* From Asian food shops and selected greengrocers.

Moroccan chicken with olives

8 free-range chicken pieces

¼ cup (60ml) olive oil

3 garlic cloves, finely
   chopped

1 tbs grated ginger

2 lemons, cut into wedges

3 tbs Moroccan spice mix*

300ml hot chicken stock

1 cup (120g) pitted green
   olives

Couscous, to serve

Preheat the oven to 180°C.

Place the chicken, oil, garlic, ginger, lemon and spice mix in a roasting pan. Season with pepper and a little salt. Using your hands, rub the spice mixture into the chicken to coat well. Roast, turning occasionally, for 45 minutes. Add the stock and olives and return to the oven, basting occasionally, for a further 15 minutes until the chicken is cooked.

Transfer the chicken to a serving dish, cover loosely with foil and set aside. Skim any excess oil from the roasting pan, then place the pan with the remaining juices and olives on the stove over medium heat. Simmer, stirring occasionally, for 5–7 minutes until thickened and reduced. Pour over the chicken, then serve with the couscous.

Serves 4

* From selected supermarkets, delis and gourmet shops.

Duck cassoulet

2 tbs olive oil

2 onions, thinly sliced

150g pancetta,
  cut into thin strips

3 tsp thyme leaves

2 garlic cloves, sliced

1 cup (250ml) dry white wine

2 x 400g cans chopped
  tomatoes

1 bay leaf

1 cup (120g) pitted green
  olives

2 x 400g cans cannellini
  beans, rinsed, drained

4 confit duck legs*

50g unsalted butter

1½ cups (105g) fresh
  breadcrumbs

2 tbs chopped flat-leaf
  parsley leaves

Mixed salad leaves, to serve

Preheat the oven to 180°C.

Heat the oil in a large saucepan over medium heat. Add the onion and pancetta, then cook, stirring, for 3–4 minutes until the onion has softened. Add the thyme, garlic and white wine, increase the heat to medium–high and bring to the boil. Simmer for 3–4 minutes until reduced by half. Add the tomatoes and bay leaf and cook for a further 10–12 minutes until reduced by one-third. Stir in the olives and cannellini beans. Season and set aside.

Scrape off any excess fat from the duck legs. (The duck fat can be kept in an airtight container in the fridge for up to 2 months. You can use it to roast potatoes.) Place the duck legs in a baking dish, pour over the sauce and cover with foil. Bake for 20 minutes or until the duck is warmed through.

Meanwhile, melt the butter in a frypan over medium heat. Add the breadcrumbs and cook, stirring, for 2–3 minutes until golden. Season, then remove from the heat and stir through the parsley.

Remove the foil from the cassoulet, scatter with the breadcrumbs, then return to the oven to bake for a further 10 minutes or until the breadcrumbs are crispy.

Divide the duck cassoulet among serving plates and serve with the mixed salad leaves. **Serves 4**

* Confit duck legs are from gourmet food shops, poultry shops and selected butchers.

Massaman roast chicken

1.5kg whole chicken

2 tbs grated ginger

2 kaffir lime leaves, finely
 shredded

2 stalks lemongrass,
 1 grated, 1 cut into thirds

2 limes, 1 halved, 1 juiced

¼ cup (70g) Massaman curry
 paste

1 tbs sunflower oil

500g small chat potatoes,
 boiled for 10 minutes,
 drained

1 cup (250ml) chicken stock

400ml coconut milk

2 tsp tamarind puree
 or paste*

1 tbs fish sauce

1 tsp grated palm sugar
 or brown sugar

2 tbs chopped unsalted
 peanuts and coriander
 sprigs, to serve

Preheat the oven to 200°C.

Rinse chicken and pat dry inside and out with paper towel. Place in an oiled roasting pan. Combine half the ginger, half the kaffir lime leaves and the grated lemongrass in a small bowl. Place in chicken cavity with halved lime and remaining 3 pieces of lemongrass. Tie chicken legs with kitchen string.

Combine 1 tbs curry paste with oil. Rub all over the chicken and season. Cover loosely with foil, then roast for 40 minutes. Remove foil, then add potatoes to the pan and baste with pan juices. Roast for a further 40 minutes or until potatoes are tender and juices run clear when the thickest part of the chicken thigh is pierced. Transfer chicken and potatoes to a serving dish, loosely cover with foil and set aside to rest.

Meanwhile, place roasting pan on the stovetop, add remaining ginger and curry paste, and stir over a low heat for 1 minute or until fragrant. Add stock and simmer for 3–4 minutes until reduced by half. Add coconut milk and simmer until reduced and thickened. Add tamarind puree, fish sauce, lime juice and sugar, then stir to combine. Pour around the chicken in the serving dish, or into a jug.

Carve chicken and serve with Massaman gravy, scattered with peanuts, coriander and remaining kaffir lime leaves. **Serves 4**

* Tamarind puree or paste is from selected supermarkets and Asian food shops.

Chicken with butter bean puree and crispy chorizo

1 tbs smoked paprika
  (pimenton)*
2 garlic cloves, finely grated
½ cup (125ml) olive oil
4 chicken breasts with skin on
  (wingbone attached –
  optional)*
400g can butter beans,
  rinsed, drained
2 fresh chorizo sausages,
  skinned and chopped
200g roasted red capsicum*,
  chopped
2 tbs chopped flat-leaf
  parsley leaves
Rocket leaves, to serve

Preheat the oven to 180°C.

Combine the paprika, garlic, 2 tablespoons olive oil and some salt and pepper in a large bowl. Add the chicken, turning to coat in the mixture, then cover and place in the fridge to marinate for 30 minutes.

Place the butter beans in a saucepan with 100ml water and warm over medium-high heat for 2–3 minutes until warmed through. Cool slightly, then place in a food processor with 3 tablespoons olive oil and some salt and pepper, then puree until smooth. Set aside.

Heat the remaining oil in a frypan over medium-high heat. Cook the chicken for 2–3 minutes each side until golden, then place on a baking tray and roast in the oven for 8–10 minutes until cooked through. Cover loosely with foil and set aside.

Meanwhile, return the frypan to medum heat, add the chorizo and cook, stirring, for 3–4 minutes until crisp. Add the capsicum, parsley and any resting juices from the chicken and toss until heated through. If necessary, gently reheat the butter bean puree over low heat. Divide the butter bean puree among serving plates, top with the chicken, then scatter with the chorizo mixture and serve garnished with the rocket. **Serves 4**

* Pimenton and roast capsicum are available from delis. Chicken breasts with skin are from poultry shops and selected butchers.

Fish pie

2 cups (500ml) milk
1 small onion, halved
2 fresh bay leaves*
3 thyme sprigs
1kg desiree or pontiac
    potatoes, peeled, chopped
100g unsalted butter
300ml thickened cream
500g skinless salmon fillet,
    pin-boned, chopped into
    3cm pieces
500g skinless white fish fillet
    (such as blue-eye or ling),
    pin-boned, chopped into
    3cm pieces
½ cup (125ml) fish stock
40g plain flour
¼ cup finely chopped flat-leaf
    parsley leaves, plus extra
    to serve
250g peeled green prawns
3 hard-boiled eggs, chopped

Place the milk, onion, bay leaves and thyme in a saucepan over medium-high heat. Bring to just below boiling point, then stand for 30 minutes to infuse. Strain into a jug, discarding the solids.

Meanwhile, preheat the oven to 180°C.

Place the potato in a saucepan of cold, salted water, bring to the boil, then reduce the heat to medium–high and cook for 12 minutes or until tender. Drain well. Pass through a potato ricer or mash well in a bowl. Add 50g butter and 200ml cream, season, then mix until smooth. Keep warm.

Place the salmon and white fish in a 1.5-litre (6-cup) baking dish and pour over the stock. Season and cover with foil. Bake for 15 minutes or until cooked through. Using a slotted spoon, transfer the fish to a bowl, reserving ⅓ cup (80ml) cooking liquid.

Melt 40g butter in a pan over medium–low heat. Add the flour and cook, stirring, for 1 minute. Gradually whisk the infused milk into the pan, then reduce the heat to low and whisk for 2–3 minutes until thickened. Whisk the reserved cooking liquid into the bechamel sauce with the remaining 100ml cream. Stir in the parsley and season.

Return the fish to the baking dish and scatter over the prawns and chopped egg. Pour over the bechamel sauce, then top with the mashed potato, smoothing out the surface with the back of a large spoon. Dot with the remaining 10g butter.

Increase the oven to 200°C. Bake the pie for 20–25 minutes until bubbling and golden. Sprinkle with the extra parsley and serve.
Serves 6

* Fresh bay leaves are from selected greengrocers.

Green curry with smoked salmon

3 kaffir lime leaves*

1 pontiac potato (about
   300g), peeled, cut into
   2cm cubes

3 tbs Thai green curry paste

300ml coconut milk

150g thin green beans,
   trimmed, cut into 4cm
   lengths

1 tbs fish sauce

1 tbs light soy sauce

Juice of 1 lime

2 tsp grated palm sugar* or
   brown sugar

4 x 175g hot-smoked salmon
   portions*, broken into
   large chunks

Jasmine rice, to serve

Finely shred 1 kaffir lime leaf and set aside to garnish. Par-cook the potato in boiling, salted water for 5 minutes. Drain.

Heat a wok or deep frypan over medium heat. Add the curry paste and stir-fry for 1 minute until fragrant. Add the coconut milk and remaining 2 lime leaves, then bring to the boil. Add the potato, turn the heat to low, then simmer for 5 minutes. Add the beans and cook for a further 2 minutes, then stir in the fish sauce, soy sauce, lime juice and sugar, adjusting to taste. Gently stir in the salmon, then cook for a further 1–2 minutes until the vegetables are tender and the salmon is heated through. Garnish with the shredded lime leaf, then serve with the rice.

Serves 4

* Kaffir lime leaves and palm sugar are from Asian food shops. Hot-smoked salmon portions are from supermarkets.

Asian-marinated baked salmon

2 lemongrass stems (pale
part only), finely chopped
½ cup (125ml) dark soy sauce
½ bunch coriander, leaves
thinly sliced, stems finely
chopped
2cm piece ginger, finely
grated
4 garlic cloves, finely grated
1kg piece skinless salmon
fillet, pin-boned (ask your
fishmonger for a whole
fillet)
⅓ cup (115g) honey, warmed
4 spring onions, finely
shredded
2 limes, halved
Mixed pea salad (we used
fresh peas, snow peas and
pea shoots), to serve

Bash the lemongrass in a mortar with a pestle until fragrant. Stir in
the soy sauce, coriander stems, ginger and garlic. Place the salmon
in a glass dish, then spread all over with the marinade. Cover and
marinate in the fridge for 1 hour.

Preheat the oven to 200°C and line a large baking tray with
baking paper. Place the salmon on the tray, then brush with the
honey. Bake for 10 minutes or until the fish is just cooked but still a
little pink in the centre.

Carefully transfer the fish to a board or serving platter, sprinkle
with the spring onion and coriander leaves, then serve warm or at
room temperature with the lime to squeeze and the pea salad.
Serves 4–6

Salmon poached in olive oil and vanilla

1L (4 cups) extra virgin
   olive oil
1 vanilla bean, split
   lengthways, seeds scraped
1–2 tarragon sprigs*
2 eschalots, sliced
4 x 120g skinless salmon
   fillets, pin-boned
Cauliflower puree or mashed
   potato, lemon wedges
   and baby spinach leaves,
   to serve

Place the olive oil, vanilla bean and seeds, tarragon and eschalot in a flameproof casserole or deep frypan (big enough to fit the salmon in a single layer) and warm gently over low heat for 3–4 minutes. Remove from the heat, then cover and stand for at least 4 hours, or overnight, for the flavours to infuse.

Season the salmon and place in the oil mixture, ensuring the fish is completely covered. Place the pan over very low heat, bring the temperature to 100°C (use a kitchen thermometer – there should be only the slightest ripple in the oil), then poach for 15 minutes. Remove the salmon from the oil with a fish slice – it will still be very pink inside but gently cooked.

Serve the salmon on the cauliflower puree or mash with the lemon wedges and spinach, drizzled with a little of the poaching oil. **Serves 4**

* Fresh tarragon is from selected greengrocers.

Mussels in cider

30g unsalted butter

4 baby or 1 large leek (white part only), thinly sliced

2 garlic cloves, finely chopped

6 bacon rashers, chopped

400ml good-quality alcoholic cider

1kg mussels, scrubbed, debearded

100g creme fraiche or sour cream

2 tbs finely chopped flat-leaf parsley leaves

Crusty bread, to serve

Melt the butter in a large saucepan over medium heat and add the leek, garlic and bacon. Cook for 5 minutes, stirring occasionally, until the leek has softened.

Add the cider and mussels and bring to a simmer. Cover with a lid and cook for 3–5 minutes until the mussels have opened. Remove and set the mussels aside, then strain the cooking liquid. Return the liquid to the pan, then place over low heat and whisk in the creme fraiche or sour cream. Stir in the parsley, then season well with salt and pepper.

Return the mussels to the pan and gently warm through over low heat, then divide among bowls and serve with the crusty bread.

Serves 4

Fish tagine

2 tbs olive oil

1 large red onion, thinly
   sliced

2 tbs chermoula paste*

400g can chopped tomatoes

1 cinnamon quill

600g good-quality
   marinara mix

½ cup green olives

1 tbs chopped coriander

Couscous and flatbread,
   to serve

Heat the oil in a large saucepan over medium heat. Add the onion and cook for 2 minutes until softened. Add the chermoula and stir for a few seconds until fragrant, then add the tomatoes, cinnamon and 350ml water. Bring to the boil, then reduce the heat to medium–low and simmer for 10 minutes until thickened. Add the seafood and simmer for a further 8–10 minutes until just cooked. Remove from the heat, stir in the olives and sprinkle with the coriander. Serve with the couscous and flatbread. **Serves 4**

* Chermoula (a North African herb and spice paste) is from Middle Eastern and gourmet shops.

Thai-style tomato soup

5 ripe tomatoes (about 750g),
   quartered
1 onion, quartered
1 tbs olive oil, plus extra to
   drizzle
2 garlic cloves, chopped
1 tsp grated ginger
1 small red chilli, seeds
   removed, chopped, plus
   thinly sliced chilli to garnish
1 bunch coriander, stems
   cleaned and chopped,
   leaves picked
½ cup (125ml) tomato juice
270ml can coconut milk
1 tbs grated palm sugar* or
   brown sugar
2 tbs fish sauce
Fried Asian shallots*, to serve

Preheat the oven to 200°C.

Place the quartered tomato and onion on a lined baking tray, drizzle with a little oil and season with salt and pepper. Roast for 30 minutes until softened.

Heat the oil in a saucepan over medium heat. Add the garlic, ginger, chilli and coriander stems and cook, stirring, for 2–3 minutes until softened. Add the tomato juice and coconut milk and bring to a simmer. Add the roasted tomato and onion with any pan juices, palm or brown sugar, fish sauce and coriander leaves (reserving some to garnish). Season and simmer over low heat for 10 minutes.

Remove the pan from the heat, then use a hand blender to puree the soup until smooth (or cool slightly, then puree in batches in a blender and return to the pan). Warm through over low heat. Ladle into serving bowls and garnish with the extra sliced chilli, reserved coriander leaves and fried Asian shallots. **Serves 4**

* Palm sugar and fried Asian shallots are from Asian food shops and selected supermarkets.

Mushroom soup with garlic bread

1 tbs olive oil, plus extra to
  drizzle
50g unsalted butter
1 garlic clove, finely chopped
1 leek, thinly sliced
1 tbs chopped thyme leaves
400g Swiss brown
  mushrooms, chopped, plus
  8 small whole mushrooms
  to serve (we used pine
  mushrooms)
10g dried porcini
  mushrooms*, soaked in
  ⅓ cup (80ml) boiling water
  for 15 minutes
3 cups (750ml) chicken stock
2 tbs soy sauce
200ml thickened cream
Garlic bread, to serve

Garlic bread
1 bagette
150g unsalted butter,
  softened
4 garlic cloves
½ cup flat-leaf parsley leaves

To make the garlic bread, slice the baguette 2cm thick, without
cutting all the way through. Whiz the remaining ingredients in a
processor with salt and pepper until well combined. Spread the
bread with garlic butter and wrap in foil.

Preheat the oven to 180°C.

Heat the oil and half the butter in a large saucepan over low heat.
Add the garlic, leek and thyme and cook, stirring, for 3–5 minutes
until the leek has softened. Add the chopped mushrooms, porcini
and soaking liquid, stock and soy sauce and bring to the boil.
Reduce the heat to low and simmer for 5–8 minutes until the
mushrooms have softened.

Place the garlic bread in the oven and bake for 10 minutes, then
open the foil and bake for 2 minutes until golden.

Remove the pan from the heat, cool slightly, then puree using a
hand blender (or puree in batches in a blender, then return to the
pan) until smooth. Add the cream and season with salt and pepper,
then warm through over low heat.

Meanwhile, melt the remaining butter in a frypan over medium
heat. Cook the small mushrooms, flat-side down, for 2–3 minutes
until just softened. Season.

To serve, ladle the soup into bowls, drizzle with the extra oil and
garnish with the pan-fried mushrooms. Serve with the garlic bread.
Serves 4–6

* Dried porcini are from delis and selected greengrocers.

Spiced carrot and lentil soup

2 tsp cumin seeds

Pinch of dried chilli flakes

2 tbs olive oil

1 onion, chopped

5 carrots (600g total), roughly
  chopped

¾ cup (150g) red lentils

1L (4 cups) chicken stock

150ml pure (thin) cream, plus
  extra to serve

Heat a large saucepan over low heat. Add the cumin and chilli flakes and cook, stirring, for 1 minute until fragrant. Remove half the spice mixture and set aside to garnish.

Increase the heat to medium and add the oil to the pan. Cook the onion, stirring, for 3–4 minutes until the onion starts to soften. Add the carrot, lentils and stock and bring to the boil. Reduce the heat to medium–low and simmer for 15–20 minutes until the carrot is tender. Cool slightly, then puree using a hand blender (or puree in batches in a blender, then return to the pan) until smooth.

Season with salt and pepper. Stir in the cream and reheat gently over low heat. Serve drizzled with the extra cream, scattered with the reserved spices. **Serves 4–6**

Cauliflower cheese soup

30g unsalted butter

1½ tbs olive oil

1 onion, chopped

1 garlic clove, chopped

1 leek, trimmed, sliced

1 small cauliflower,
  broken into florets

3 cups (750ml) chicken stock

100g grated cheddar cheese

1–2 tsp wholegrain mustard

300ml thickened cream

4 slices flat pancetta*
  or bacon

½ cup (35g) fresh
  breadcrumbs

2 tbs chopped chives

Cheddar wafers

¾ cup (90g) finely
  grated cheddar cheese

2 tbs plain flour

Preheat the oven to 180°C. Line 2 large baking trays with foil.

Melt the butter with 1 tablespoon oil in a frypan over medium heat. Cook the onion, garlic and leek, stirring, for 3–4 minutes until soft but not coloured. Add the cauliflower and stock, bring to the boil, then reduce the heat to medium–low and simmer for 20 minutes or until the cauliflower is tender. Cool slightly, then stir in the cheddar, mustard and half the cream.

In batches, blend the cauliflower soup until smooth. Return to a clean saucepan. Add the remaining 150ml cream, season, then stir over low heat to warm through.

Meanwhile, for the cheddar wafers, combine the cheddar and flour in a bowl and season. Place twelve 5cm rounds of the cheddar mixture on the lined baking trays, leaving room between each to spread. Bake for 5–6 minutes until golden. Set aside to cool.

Place the pancetta on a baking tray and bake for 6–8 minutes until crispy. Cool slightly, then break into small pieces.

Place the breadcrumbs on a baking tray and drizzle with the remaining 2 teaspoons oil. Place in the oven and bake for 5–6 minutes until golden and crispy.

Ladle the soup into serving bowls, then top with the pancetta, chives and breadcrumbs. Serve the soup with the cheddar wafers.
Serves 4–6

* Flat pancetta is from delis.

Tomato soup with spaghetti and chicken meatballs

1 tbs olive oil

1 onion, thinly sliced

2 garlic cloves, finely
chopped

1 tbs tomato paste

2 x 400g cans chopped
tomatoes

1.25L (5 cups) chicken stock

500g thin chicken sausages

100g spaghetti, broken into
5cm lengths

Chopped basil, grated
parmesan cheese and
crusty bread, to serve

Heat the oil in a large saucepan over medium heat. Add the onion and cook for 2–3 minutes, stirring, until softened. Add the garlic and tomato paste and cook, stirring, for a further 1 minute. Add the tomatoes and 2½ cups (625ml) of the chicken stock. Bring to the boil, then reduce the heat to low and simmer for 20 minutes while you make the meatballs.

For the meatballs, place the remaining 2½ cups (625ml) chicken stock in a saucepan and bring to the boil. Squeeze the sausage meat from the casings and form into about 30 small (3cm) meatballs. Add the meatballs to the stock and simmer for 10 minutes until cooked through. Remove meatballs to a plate with a slotted spoon, then return stock to the boil. Add the spaghetti and cook until al dente. Drain, discarding the stock.

Use a hand blender to blend the soup until smooth (or blend in batches in a blender, then return to the pan). Add the cooked spaghetti and meatballs to the soup and warm through gently for 5 minutes over low heat. Ladle the soup into bowls, garnish with the basil and parmesan, then serve with the bread. **Serves 4–6**

Asian chicken and coconut soup

3 cups (750ml) good quality
   chicken stock
3 cups (750ml) coconut milk
3cm piece ginger, peeled,
   cut into matchsticks
2 lemongrass stems, bruised
2 long red chillies, sliced
8 kaffir lime leaves*
175g mixed Asian mushrooms
   (such as shiitake, shimeji
   and enoki)*, trimmed
2 chicken breasts, thinly
   sliced
¼ cup (60ml) fish sauce
⅓ cup (80ml) lime juice, plus
   lime wedges to serve
2 tsp grated palm sugar* or
   brown sugar
Coriander leaves, to garnish

Place the chicken stock, coconut milk, ginger, lemongrass, chilli and 6 kaffir lime leaves in a saucepan. Bring to the boil, then reduce the heat to medium–low and simmer for 5 minutes to infuse.

Add the mushrooms and chicken, then cook for a further 5 minutes until the chicken is cooked through and the mushrooms are tender. Add the fish sauce, lime juice and sugar, then adjust seasoning to taste.

Finely shred the remaining kaffir lime leaves. Divide the soup among bowls, then serve garnished with the coriander and shredded kaffir lime leaf, with lime wedges to squeeze over.
Serves 4–6

* From Asian food shops and selected greengrocers.

Pea soup with croque monsieur

1 tbs olive oil

20g unsalted butter

1 onion, chopped

2 celery stalks, chopped

1 leek (pale part only), thinly
sliced

1 potato, peeled, chopped

1 bouquet garni*

2 cups (500ml) chicken stock

2 cups (240g) frozen peas
(not baby)

½ cup (125ml) pure (thin)
cream

Toasted croque monsieur
sandwiches* or croutons,
to serve

Snow pea sprouts, to garnish

Heat the oil and butter in a saucepan over medium heat. Add the onion, celery and leek and cook, stirring, for 5 minutes or until the vegetables are soft but not browned. Add the potato, bouquet garni and stock and simmer for 5 minutes until the potato is soft. Add the peas and cream and simmer for a further minute, then remove 2–3 tablespoons peas with a slotted spoon and set aside.

Puree using a hand blender (or puree in batches in a blender, then return to the pan) until smooth. Return the reserved peas to the pan and reheat the soup gently over low heat. Serve the soup in bowls with a croque monsieur in the centre, if desired, garnished with the snow pea sprouts. **Serves 4–6**

* Bouquet garni is a bunch of herbs (usually parsley, thyme and bay leaves) tied with string and used to flavour soups and stews. Make your own fresh, or buy ready-made dried bouquet garni from delis and selected supermarkets. A toasted croque monsieur sandwich is filled with ham, mustard and gruyere cheese.

Eggplant and chickpea curry

1 large eggplant (about 500g)

1 tbs sunflower oil

1 onion, chopped

2 tbs medium curry powder

400g can chopped tomatoes

400g can chickpeas, rinsed,
  drained

150g baby spinach leaves

2 tbs mango chutney,
  plus extra to serve

Steamed basmati rice and
  pappadams, to serve

Preheat the oven to 200°C.

Prick the eggplant all over with a fork and place on a baking tray. Roast for 30 minutes or until tender and starting to wilt. Cool slightly.

Meanwhile, place the oil in a deep frypan (with a lid) over medium heat. Add the onion and cook, stirring, for 2–3 minutes until softened. Add the curry powder and cook, stirring, for 1 minute. Stir in the tomatoes, chickpeas and 200ml water, then reduce the heat to low, cover and simmer for 10 minutes or until fragrant.

Chop the eggplant and stir into the curry with the spinach and mango chutney. Cook, uncovered, for 2–3 minutes until the spinach has wilted. Season, then serve with the rice, pappadams and extra mango chutney. **Serves 4**

Baked mushrooms with pine nuts and feta

1 tbs olive oil, plus extra to
  drizzle
1 onion, finely chopped
3 garlic cloves, finely
  chopped
1½ cups (105g) fresh
  breadcrumbs
50g Persian (marinated) feta*,
  crumbled
1 long red chilli, seeds
  removed, finely chopped
2 tbs finely chopped flat-leaf
  parsley leaves
2 tbs pine nuts, toasted
4 portobello or other large
  flat mushrooms
300g Roman beans* or green
  beans, trimmed
1 cup (250ml) good-quality
  tomato pasta sauce

Preheat the oven to 180°C.

Heat the oil in a frypan over medium heat. Add the onion and cook, stirring, for 2–3 minutes until softened. Add the garlic and cook for 30 seconds, then transfer to a bowl with the breadcrumbs, feta, chilli, parsley and pine nuts. Season well, then stir to combine.

Place the mushrooms on a baking tray, cup-side up, then fill with the breadcrumb mixture. Drizzle with a little extra oil and bake for 15 minutes or until the mushrooms are cooked and the filling is golden brown.

Meanwhile, blanch the beans in a saucepan of boiling, salted water for 2–3 minutes until just tender. Drain, then refresh.

Place the pasta sauce in a frypan over medium–low heat and gently warm through. Toss the beans in the sauce and serve with the mushrooms. **Serves 4**

* Persian feta is from delis and supermarkets. Roman beans are from selected greengrocers.

Pumpkin, goat's cheese and onion marmalade jalousie

700g pumpkin, peeled, cut
   into 2cm pieces
1 tbs olive oil
1 tbs chopped rosemary
   leaves
2 x 375g blocks frozen puff
   pastry, thawed
375g jar onion marmalade*
150g soft goat's cheese
1 egg, beaten

Preheat the oven to 200°C.

Spread the pumpkin on a lined baking tray and toss with the olive oil, salt and pepper. Sprinkle with the rosemary and roast for 30 minutes or until tender. Cool.

Reduce the oven to 180°C. Roll out 1 block of pastry on a lightly floured surface to form a 20cm x 30cm rectangle. Place on a lined baking tray and prick the base in several places with a fork, leaving a 2cm border. Spread the base inside the border with two-thirds of the onion marmalade, then top with the pumpkin and goat's cheese. Season with salt and pepper. Brush the pastry border with the egg.

Roll out the second block of pastry slightly larger than the first. Fold the pastry in half lengthways and use a sharp knife to make cuts in the folded side, about 1cm apart and leaving a 2cm border on the unfolded side. Carefully open the pastry back out and place over the filling, pressing to seal the edges – the cuts in the pastry should separate slightly to reveal some of the filling. Trim the edges if necessary, then brush all over with the egg. Bake for 30 minutes or until puffed and golden, then serve with the remaining onion marmalade. **Serves 4–6**

* From delis and gourmet food shops.

Twice-baked soufflés

50g unsalted butter

½ cup (75g) plain flour

2 cups (500ml) milk

Pinch of grated nutmeg

4 eggs, separated, plus 1
   extra eggwhite

150g baby spinach leaves,
   blanched, squeezed dry

120g soft goat's cheese,
   crumbled

½ cup (40g) finely grated
   parmesan cheese

½ cup (125ml) pure (thin)
   cream

⅓ cup (35g) toasted walnuts

Micro salad leaves*, to serve

Preheat the oven to 180°C and grease six 1-cup (250ml) dariole moulds or ovenproof teacups.

Melt the butter in a saucepan over low heat and add the flour. Cook, stirring, for 1 minute. Whisk in the milk, nutmeg and some salt and pepper. Bring to just below boiling point, then whisk for 2 minutes or until very thick and smooth. Add the egg yolks, one at a time, beating well after each addition. Stir in the spinach, goat's cheese and half the parmesan.

In a clean, dry bowl, whisk the 5 eggwhites with a pinch of salt until soft peaks form. Fold one-third of the eggwhite into the cheese mixture to loosen, then fold in the remaining eggwhite until just combined.

Place the moulds in a baking dish and divide the soufflé mixture among them. Run your finger around the inside edge of the mould (this will ensure the soufflés will rise evenly), then pour enough boiling water into the pan to come halfway up the sides of the moulds. Bake in the oven for 15–20 minutes until puffed and golden. Remove the moulds from the baking dish, cool, then invert onto a greased baking tray. The soufflés can be chilled at this stage for up to 24 hours, if desired.

When almost ready to serve, preheat the oven to 180°C.

Pour the cream over the soufflés and sprinkle with the remaining ¼ cup (20g) parmesan. Bake the soufflés for 10–12 minutes until puffed and golden. Scatter with the walnuts and salad leaves and serve immediately. **Makes 6**

* Micro salad leaves are from farmers' markets and selected greengrocers.

Goat's cheese, roast capsicum and spinach lasagne

400g baby spinach leaves
200ml creme fraiche or light
   sour cream
100g pure (thin) cream
2 eggs, beaten
½ cup (40g) grated parmesan
   cheese
750g roast capsicum pieces*,
   drained
250g soft goat's cheese
375g fresh lasagne sheets
Green salad, to serve

Preheat the oven to 190°C.

Blanch the spinach for 1 minute in boiling water until wilted. Drain in a sieve, pressing down to remove excess liquid. Cool.

Combine the creme fraiche, cream, eggs and half the parmesan in a bowl. Season with salt and pepper.

Pat the roast capsicum with paper towel to remove excess oil. Spread one-third of the cream mixture over the base of a 20cm x 26cm (1.5 litre/6 cups) baking dish, cover with half the capsicum, crumble over half the goat's cheese, then layer with half the spinach. Cover with a layer of pasta sheets, cutting to fit. Repeat the layers, then finish with a final layer of cream mixture. Sprinkle with the remaining parmesan, then cover with baking paper and foil.

Bake for 30 minutes, then remove the paper and foil and bake for a further 10–15 minutes until the top is golden and bubbling. Stand for 5 minutes, then slice and serve with a green salad. **Serves 4–6**

* From supermarkets and delis.

Mushroom and potato tarts

20g dried porcini
   mushrooms*
3 frozen, thawed shortcrust
   pastry sheets
2 potatoes (about 400g),
   peeled
2 eggs
1 cup (240g) creme fraiche
2 tsp chopped thyme leaves
¼ cup (65g) soft goat's
   cheese, crumbled
30g unsalted butter
1 tbs olive oil
1 garlic clove, finely chopped
300g mixed fresh mushrooms
   (such as Swiss brown and
   chestnut), sliced if large
2 tbs chopped flat-leaf
   parsley leaves
Salad leaves, to serve

Soak the dried porcini in ½ cup (125ml) boiling water for
30 minutes. Drain, squeezing out excess liquid, then roughly chop
the porcini and set aside.

Use the pastry to line six 12cm loose-bottomed tart pans,
trimming any excess. Chill for 15 minutes.

Place the potatoes in a saucepan of cold, salted water. Bring to
the boil over medium-high heat, then cook for 8–10 minutes to
par-boil. Cool, then slice into thin rounds.

Preheat the oven to 180°C.

Line the tart shells with baking paper and fill with pastry weights
or uncooked rice. Bake for 10 minutes, then remove the paper and
weights and bake for a further 2–3 minutes or until golden and dry.
Cool slightly.

Whisk the eggs, creme fraiche and 1 teaspoon thyme together,
then season. Arrange the potato slices, slightly overlapping, in the
tart shells and pour over the creme fraiche mixture. Scatter with the
goat's cheese and bake for 15 minutes or until the filling is set.

Meanwhile, place the butter and oil in a frypan over medium-high
heat. Add the garlic, fresh mushrooms and the remaining
1 teaspoon thyme, then cook, stirring, for 3–4 minutes until
softened. Add the porcini and parsley, then season and cook for a
further 2–3 minutes until tender.

Top the tarts with the mushroom mixture and serve with the salad
leaves. **Serves 6**

* Dried porcini are from delis and gourmet food shops.

110

Porcini and chicken liver pâté

20g dried porcini
   mushrooms*
450g chicken livers, cleaned,
   trimmed
1 cup (250ml) milk
150g unsalted butter,
   softened
1 red onion, finely chopped
2 garlic cloves, finely
   chopped
2 tsp chopped thyme leaves
2 pancetta slices, chopped
2 tbs brandy
200g redcurrant jelly
Baguette, to serve

Place the porcini in a bowl with ½ cup (125ml) boiling water and soak for 30 minutes. Place the chicken livers in a bowl, cover with the milk and soak for 30 minutes – this will result in a milder flavour.

Drain the porcini, reserving the soaking liquid, and chop. Drain the livers, discarding the milk, and set aside.

Melt 25g butter in a frypan over medium heat. Cook the onion, garlic, thyme, chopped porcini and soaking liquid, stirring, for 3–4 minutes until the liquid evaporates. Season, then remove from the pan and set aside.

Add 25g butter to the pan and increase the heat to medium–high. Cook livers and pancetta, turning, for 3–4 minutes until the livers are browned on the outside, but still pink in the middle. Add the brandy and cook for 1 minute, then return the onion mixture to the pan, stirring to combine. Remove from the heat and cool.

Whiz the liver mixture in a blender with the remaining 100g butter until smooth. Press the pâté through a sieve, then spoon into four 1 cup (250ml) ramekins or jars. Cover, then chill for 30 minutes or until firm.

Melt the redcurrant jelly in a small saucepan over low heat. Cool slightly, then pour over each pâté and chill for at least 1 hour or until set. Remove from the fridge 30 minutes before serving.

Bring the pâtés back to room temperature, then serve with some crusty baguette. **Serves 4**

* From gourmet food shops and greengrocers.

tartiflette on toast

2 large potatoes, peeled,
cut into 2cm cubes
1 tbs olive oil
4 bacon rashers, chopped
⅓ cup (80ml) dry white wine
1 tsp chopped thyme leaves
⅓ cup (80g) creme fraiche
or sour cream
4 slices sourdough bread
8 slices gruyere or
cheddar cheese
Bitter salad leaves, to serve

Cook the potato in boiling, salted water for 3 minutes or until just tender. Drain.

Meanwhile, heat the oil in a frypan over medium heat. Add the bacon and cook, stirring, for 3–4 minutes until starting to crisp. Add the potato and cook, stirring, for 1–2 minutes until the potato starts to colour. Add the wine and allow to bubble for 2–3 minutes until it has evaporated, then stir in the thyme and creme fraiche. Season the tartiflette with sea salt and freshly ground black pepper.

Preheat the grill to high. Toast the bread on both sides, then top with the tartiflette and the cheese. Grill for 1–2 minutes until the cheese is bubbling and melted. Season with freshly ground pepper. Serve with a salad of bitter leaves. **Serves 4**

Bagna cauda with baby vegetables

2 cups (500ml) pure (thin)
  cream
6 garlic cloves
20g unsalted butter
10 anchovy fillets, drained
½ cup (35g) fresh
  breadcrumbs
Extra virgin olive oil, to
  drizzle
Chargrilled ciabatta, to serve
Blanched baby vegetables
  (such as baby carrots,
  golden and red baby
  beetroots, baby zucchini
  and cauliflower florets),
  to dip

Place the cream and garlic cloves in a small saucepan over medium heat. Bring to a simmer, then reduce the heat to low and cook for 15–20 minutes until the cream has reduced by half. Cool slightly.

Meanwhile, melt the butter in a separate saucepan over medium–low heat, add the anchovies and gently heat for 1–2 minutes, stirring, until the anchovies start to dissolve.

Place the cream, garlic, anchovies, butter and breadcrumbs in a blender and blend until smooth.

Spoon the warm bagna cauda into a bowl. Drizzle with the olive oil, season with freshly ground black pepper and serve with the grilled ciabatta and blanched baby vegetables. **Serves 6–8**

Instant fondue with roast vegetables

2 red capsicums

2 yellow capsicums

2 zucchini

1 small kumara (about 200g), peeled

6 garlic cloves (unpeeled)

2 tbs olive oil, plus extra to drizzle

12 thyme sprigs

300g wheel camembert or brie

Crusty bread, to serve

Preheat the oven to 190°C.

Cut the capsicums, zucchini and kumara into 2cm pieces. Place in a bowl with the garlic cloves and toss with the oil. Spread the vegetables in a baking dish and scatter with the thyme. Drizzle with a little more oil and bake, turning once, for 20–25 minutes until softened and just starting to brown.

Meanwhile, use a sharp knife to score a cross in the centre of the cheese rind. Place in the dish with the vegetables, then return to the oven for a further 5 minutes until the cheese starts to ooze and melt. Serve in the baking dish, with forks so everyone can dip their vegetables and crusty bread. **Serves 4–6**

Autumn rosti with hot-smoked salmon

1 kumara (about 330g)

1 large potato (about 250g)

½ small carrot (about 75g)

1 small parsnip (about 150g)

¼ tsp grated or ground
nutmeg

2 tbs finely chopped thyme
leaves

1 egg

20g unsalted butter

1 tbs olive oil

⅓ cup (80g) creme fraiche
or sour cream

2 tbs grated lemon zest,
plus extra to sprinkle

175g hot-smoked salmon
portion*, flaked

2 tbs finely chopped chives

Peel all the vegetables and cut into 4cm pieces. Place in a saucepan of cold, salted water and bring to the boil. Blanch for 4 minutes until just tender, then drain and allow to cool.

Coarsely grate all the vegetables into a large bowl, then add the nutmeg, thyme and egg, season well and stir to combine. Form into 12 patties, then chill for 15 minutes.

Place half the butter and 2 teaspoons oil in a frypan over medium heat. Add half the patties and cook for 1–2 minutes each side until golden and crisp. Keep warm in a low oven while you repeat with the remaining butter, oil and vegetable mixture.

Combine the creme fraiche with the lemon zest and some salt and pepper.

To serve, divide the rosti among plates, top with a dollop of creme fraiche and some smoked salmon, then sprinkle with the chives and extra lemon zest. **Makes 12**

* Available from supermarkets and delis.

Warm barley and mushroom salad with Taleggio

⅔ cup (150g) pearl barley

10g dried porcini
   mushrooms*

50g unsalted butter

⅓ cup (80ml) extra virgin
   olive oil

1 garlic clove, finely chopped

350g mixed wild mushrooms
   (such as chestnut, shiitake
   and Swiss browns), sliced
   or left whole

⅓ cup finely chopped
   flat-leaf parsley leaves

2 tbs chopped chives

⅓ cup finely chopped
   mint leaves

1 tbs red wine vinegar

1 bunch rocket

150g Taleggio cheese*, sliced

Place the barley in a saucepan of cold water over medium-high heat. Bring to the boil, then reduce the heat to low and cook for 1 hour or until the barley is tender, topping up the water if necessary. Drain.

Meanwhile, soak the porcini in ½ cup (125ml) boiling water for 10 minutes. Drain, reserving the soaking liquid, then roughly chop the porcini and set aside.

Melt the butter with 1 tablespoon oil in a frypan over medium heat. Add the garlic and wild mushrooms, then cook, stirring occasionally, for 3–4 minutes until tender. Add the porcini and soaking liquid, then cook for a further 2–3 minutes until most of the liquid has been absorbed. Toss the mushrooms and herbs with the barley and season. Keep warm.

Whisk the remaining ¼ cup (60ml) olive oil with the red wine vinegar, season, then toss with the rocket.

Fold the Taleggio through the warm barley salad, then divide among serving plates. Top with the dressed rocket and serve.

Serves 6

* Dried porcini mushrooms and Taleggio cheese (an Italian washed-rind cheese) are available from delis.

Deep-fried brie with sweet chilli sauce

2 cups panko* breadcrumbs
  or coarse fresh
  breadcrumbs
Finely grated zest of 1 lemon
2 tbs chopped flat-leaf
  parsley leaves
2 tbs plain flour
1 egg, beaten
2 tbs milk
350g piece brie or
  camembert, cut into
  4 wedges
Sunflower oil, to deep-fry
Sweet chilli sauce and wild
  rocket leaves, to serve

Place the breadcrumbs in a food processor with the lemon zest and parsley, then pulse to fine crumbs. Place the crumb mixture in a shallow bowl, place the flour in a separate bowl, and gently whisk the egg and milk in a third bowl.

Toss the wedges of cheese first in the flour, shaking off excess, then in the egg mixture, then in the breadcrumbs. Place on a plate and chill for at least 30 minutes (or up to 4 hours ahead).

Half-fill a deep-fryer or large heavy-based saucepan with oil and heat to 190°C. (If you don't have a deep-fryer thermometer, test a cube of bread – it'll turn golden in 30 seconds when the oil is hot enough.) Deep-fry the cheese for 1 minute or until golden all over, then drain briefly on paper towel. Serve immediately with the sweet chilli sauce and rocket. **Serves 4**

* Coarse, light Japanese breadcrumbs from Asian food shops.

Index

ABC
Books

The ABC 'Wave' device is a trademark of the
Australian Broadcasting Corporation and is used under
licence by HarperCollins*Publishers* Australia.
The *delicious.* trademark is used under licence from the
Australian Broadcasting Corporation and NewsLifeMedia.

delicious. Slow comprises recipes and photographs originally published in *delicious.*
Faking It (2008), *delicious. Quick Smart Cook* (2009), *delicious. More Please* (2010), *delicious.*
Simply the Best (2011), *delicious. Home Cooking* (2012) and *delicious. Love to Cook* (2013)

First published in Australia in 2014
by HarperCollins*Publishers* Australia Pty Limited
ABN 36 009 913 517
harpercollins.com.au

HarperCollins*Publishers*
Level 13, 201 Elizabeth Street, Sydney NSW 2000, Australia
Unit D1, 63 Apollo Drive, Rosedale, Auckland 0632 New Zealand
A 53, Sector 57, Noida, UP, India
1London Bridge Street, London SE1 9GF, United Kingdom
2 Bloor Street East, 20th floor, Toronto, Ontario M4W 1A8, Canada
195 Broadway, New York, NY 10007, USA

National Library of Australia Cataloguing-in-Publication data:
Little, Valli, author.
  Delicious: slow / Valli Little.
  ISBN: 978 0 7333 3339 2 (pbk)
  Cooking.
641.5

Photography by Brett Stevens, Ian Wallace, Jeremy Simons
Styling by David Morgan, Louise Pickford
Cover and internal design by Hazel Lam, HarperCollins Design Studio
Typesetting by Judi Rowe, Agave Creative Group
Colour reproduction by Graphic Print Group, Adelaide, SA

Printed and bound in China by RR Donnelley

8 7 6 5   15 16 17 18